OCS

150

Elizabeth Bloomer Ford

Elizabeth Bloomer Ford

✦✦✦✦✦✦✦✦✦✦✦✦✦✦✦✦✦✦✦✦

1918–

BY DAN SANTOW

CHILDREN'S PRESS®
A Division of Grolier Publishing
New York   London   Hong Kong   Sydney
Danbury, Connecticut

Consultant:	LINDA CORNWELL
	Coordinator of School Quality and Professional Improvement
	Indiana State Teachers Association

Project Editor:	DOWNING PUBLISHING SERVICES
Page Layout:	CAROLE DESNOES
Photo Researcher:	JAN IZZO

Visit Children's Press on the Internet at:
http://publishing.grolier.com

Library of Congress Cataloging-in-Publication Data
Santow, Dan.
    Elizabeth Bloomer Ford, 1918– / by Dan Santow
       p. cm. — (Encyclopedia of first ladies)
    Includes bibliographical references and index.
    Summary: A biography of the wife of the thirty-eighth president of the United States, a relaxed, friendly White House hostess who supported women's rights and helped raise breast cancer awareness by talking openly about her own surgery.
    ISBN 0-516-20641-9
    1. Ford, Betty, 1918– Juvenile literature. 2. Presidents' spouses—United States—Biography—Juvenile literature. [1. Ford, Betty, 1918– 2. First ladies. 3. Women—Biography]
I. Title   II. Series
E867.S26   2000
973.925'092—dc 21   99–16786
[B]   CIP
                                                     AC

Table of Contents

Elizabeth Bloomer Ford

CHAPTER ONE

As Fate Would Have It

☆ ☆ ☆ ☆ ☆ ☆ ☆ ☆ ☆ ☆ ☆ ☆ ☆ ☆ ☆ ☆

Everyone kept asking Betty Ford what she was going to do with her hair, as if a new curl, a new style, or a new shade of ash brown, would transform her into the perfect vice president's wife.

It was October 1973, and Betty's husband, Congressman Jerry Ford, had just been appointed by President Richard Nixon to be his new second-in-command. The current vice president, Spiro Agnew, had resigned. There was talk that whomever was appointed to the office might soon take over the presidency if Richard Nixon's legal problems continued. That meant Betty Ford might become First Lady!

☆ ☆ ☆ ☆ ☆ ☆ ☆ ☆ ☆ ☆ ☆ ☆ ☆ ☆ ☆ ☆

President Richard M. Nixon and Congressman Gerald R. Ford conferring at the time Ford became Nixon's choice for vice president

The Nixons and the Fords pose in the White House Blue Room following the nomination of Gerald Ford as Nixon's choice to succeed Spiro Agnew as vice president.

A Vice President Resigns

Many Americans were surprised when presidential candidate Richard Nixon chose Spiro T. Agnew as his running mate in the election of 1968. Little was known about Agnew, the governor of Maryland, except that he was extremely conservative. However, at a time when the Vietnam War and civil-rights issues had seriously divided the nation, Spiro Agnew's stands against student antiwar protests, black activism, the press, and liberal thinking had a certain appeal. "Spiro Is My Hero" read bumper stickers on the cars of his conservative supporters. But Agnew turned out to be controversial for more than his politics. In 1973, the Justice Department uncovered

evidence that as governor, Agnew had accepted money from companies in exchange for work from the state. Evidence suggested that he even took bribes as vice president. He also faced charges of not paying income taxes. As part of a plea bargain, Agnew agreed to resign the vice presidency. He served three months probation and paid a $10,000 fine. Only one other vice president has ever resigned the office. In 1832, John C. Calhoun left the service of President Andrew Jackson to become a senator.

Betty and Vice President Gerald Ford on December 8, 1973

The First Lady received more attention than any other politician's wife, and especially more than the vice president's wife. The attention came from the press, of course, but especially from women, who looked to her as inspiration for everything from politics to fashion.

IN GOD WE TRUST

Newly sworn-in Vice President Gerald R. Ford kisses his wife Betty to the applause of President Nixon and the joint session of Congress, December 6, 1973.

13

Betty Ford, always a wife and mother first, a political wife second, made sure she was there for her children. The Fords are shown here with their sons Jack and Mike during a skiing vacation in 1959.

Betty Ford had been in the public eye to some extent during the many years Jerry had served as a powerful congressman from Grand Rapids, Michigan. Yet there was never any question in her mind that she was always a mother and wife first, a political wife second. What she thought on this issue or that, what she wore to a PTA meeting or even to a party honoring a visiting foreign dignitary, was far less important than being there when her children returned from school or spending time each Christmas skiing with the family in Vail.

The role of First Lady had changed much since Martha Washington struggled with her role as the wife of the first president of the United States 200 years before.

As recently as twenty years earlier, Bess Truman, the wife of President Harry Truman, never spoke to the press and was rarely photographed in all her finery. Even the current First Lady, Pat Nixon, was well known not for her views or style but for her desire for privacy, for wanting as little publicity about herself and her family as possible.

And now it had come true. Only eight months after Gerald Rudolph Ford had officially become vice presi-

Top: First Lady Bess Truman never spoke to the press and rarely sat for formal photographs. Bottom: First Lady Pat Nixon protected the privacy of her family as much as possible.

Watergate

✫ ✫

In June 1972, President Richard Nixon was campaigning for reelection against Democratic opponent George McGovern. On June 17, five men were caught breaking into the headquarters of the Democratic National Committee in the Watergate, a hotel and office complex in Washington, D.C. Authorities discovered that high-ranking members of President Nixon's reelection committee had sent the intruders to bug the Democratic offices. A massive investigation followed, and scandal erupted. Though Nixon won reelection, by March 1974, he was strongly linked with attempts to cover up the break-in. When it became known that the president had a secret recording system in the White House, Special Prosecutor Archibald Cox subpoenaed the tape recordings, hoping to hear the president and his staff discussing a cover-up of the Watergate break-in. President Nixon refused to hand over the tapes. It wasn't until the Supreme Court ruled that he must turn over the tapes as evidence that President Nixon released some of the recordings. They revealed no hard evidence but did contain a suspicious 18-minute gap. Meanwhile, more and more members of Nixon's staff were facing criminal charges for their roles in the break-in and cover-up. In August 1974, Nixon finally released tapes that connected him to cover-up attempts. To avoid impeachment, the president resigned on August 9, the only American president to leave office voluntarily. Among his firsts acts as president, Gerald Ford pardoned Nixon of any wrongdoing in the Watergate affair.

dent, Nixon had resigned. "Up until then," said Betty, "I kept hoping something would happen that would save the president, save the office, save all of us—hoping it wouldn't end the way it ended."

There was no savior, and now as never before Betty Ford had a lot more than her hair to worry about. A few months ago, she had finally convinced Jerry to retire from politics so they could spend more time together. Now

he was going to be president and she would be the First Lady!

The idea sent shivers down Betty's spine.

In fact, there had already been one heated controversy. Betty had stated that she and Jerry would not have separate bedrooms in the White House, as had most previous presidents and First Ladies. She even added that they were going to take their own bed with them to the White House. People ac-

Earth Tones and Leisure Suits

✫ ✫

As a former fashion model, Betty Ford's sense of style tended toward the classic and conservative. Her good taste protected her from some of the more outlandish fashion statements of the 1970s. Platform shoes, hot pants, and thigh-high boots would hardly have suited the First Lady. Even though designers introduced mid-calf-length ("midi") skirts in 1970, American women continued to bare their knees in miniskirts. The spell of miniskirts would not be entirely broken until 1977 when the star of the movie *Annie Hall* triggered a new look for women with her baggy trousers, long skirts, and tweed jackets. Generally, fashion in the 1970s grew more casual, and colors tended toward the earth tones of brown, orange, and beige. The youth uniform of blue jeans and T-shirts spread into the mainstream, and high fashion designers made "designer blue jeans" popular. Working women flexed their feminist muscle by wearing pantsuits, though many conservative workplaces still frowned on such a masculine look for their women employees. Disco lovers and grandfathers alike adopted the "leisure suit," a creatively colored casual jacket and slacks usually made of polyester and worn without a tie. Nike introduced its first athletic shoes in 1972, and as people's interest in fitness began to grow, jogging suits became popular on and off the track. Perhaps the greatest fashion statement of the 1970s occurred, however, when Beverly Johnson graced the cover of *Vogue* in 1974, the first black model to appear on the cover of a major fashion magazine.

cused her of being "disgraceful and immoral."

"I didn't care," Betty said. "I wanted to be a good First Lady, I was perfectly willing to be educated about the duties of a First Lady, but I didn't believe I had to do every single thing some previous president's wife had done."

Of more importance, what would be her issues while she lived in the White House? What sort of White

House would she create? What sort of personal style would she want to project? And how could she maintain her sense of self when everything she uttered would be weighed and dissected in the press? These were all important questions that eventually would have to be answered carefully and in detail.

But not just yet. It was Inauguration Day now, the morning of the most momentous day in their lives, and Betty just wanted to stay in control. Every morning she studied a verse out of a pamphlet called *Forward Day by Day*, and this morning would be no different. The recommended verse from the *Living Bible* had said, "I will keep a muzzle on my mouth."

"Ordinarily, I'm hard to muzzle," said Betty. On that day, however, "if you'd asked me my name, I'd have been stuck for an answer."

There were, of course, many things about which to worry. First, the family had to get to the swearing-in ceremonies—which was easier said than done.

Their four children were all around the country and had to be rounded up: Mike and his wife Gayle were on the way to Boston with their wedding presents. When they arrived, a secret service man gave them plane tickets to return to Washington immediately. Jack was a forest ranger at Yellowstone National Park, and he had to be airlifted out by a helicopter.

Finally, they were together: "an accidental president," as Betty had called Jerry, an accidental First Lady, as she might have called herself, and the family.

On the morning Jerry was to take his oath of office, a limousine took the family to the vice president's office. There, they watched on television in solemn quiet as the Nixon family said good-bye to their friends and staff. Then the same limousine took them all to the White House. Jerry and Betty walked with the Nixons, their good friends and political colleagues, to the waiting helicopter on the lawn of the White House.

"My heavens, they've even rolled out the red carpet for us," Pat Nixon said to Betty as they neared the helicopter. "Well, Betty, you'll see many of these red carpets and you'll get so you'll hate them."

Vice President Gerald Ford and his wife Betty walk down a red carpet with President Richard Nixon and First Lady Pat Nixon on the way to the helicopter that would take the Nixons away from the White House.

As they walked between the two rows of military men, they stopped halfway up the carpet. It was 11 o'clock in the morning and President Nixon shook Jerry Ford's hand one last time. Jerry looked him straight in the eye and said, "Good-bye, Mr. President."

With that, the Nixons entered the helicopter and were flown away, like a bird disappearing into the horizon.

An hour later, the Ford family was together again to witness with the entire world the swearing-in of Gerald Rudolph (Jerry) Ford as thirty-eighth president of the United States. Betty stood beside him, holding the Bible during his oath. It was opened to a fa-

Vice President Gerald Ford was sworn in as president of the United States by Chief Justice Warren E. Burger on August 9, 1974.

During the swearing-in ceremony, Betty Ford held a Bible opened to a favorite passage of hers.

The Ford family gathered in the Oval Office for a photograph after Ford was sworn in as president. From left: sons Jack and Steve, Betty, Gerald, daughter Susan, daughter-in-law Gayle, and son Mike.

vorite passage of hers: "Trust in the Lord with all thine heart; and lean not unto thine own understanding."

As Jerry repeated the oath of office as president of the United States, Betty thought that she, too, was taking an oath, "promising to dedicate my own life to the service of my country."

After the ceremony, she and the family, along with their friends and other well-wishers, gathered at their home to celebrate.

"The morning had begun with tears, lives being broken, people being broken," wrote Betty, "and now there was laughter, and everybody from Crown View Drive was in our kitchen eating ham and salad and lasagna and wishing us well and toasting the new president, and Jerry was in his shirt-sleeves, pouring champagne."

It was exhausting *and* exhilarating. "That night I lay in the dark and stared at the ceiling," wrote Betty. "My God, I thought, what a job I have to do."

☆ ☆ ☆ ☆ ☆ ☆ ☆ ☆ ☆ ☆ ☆ ☆ ☆ ☆ ☆

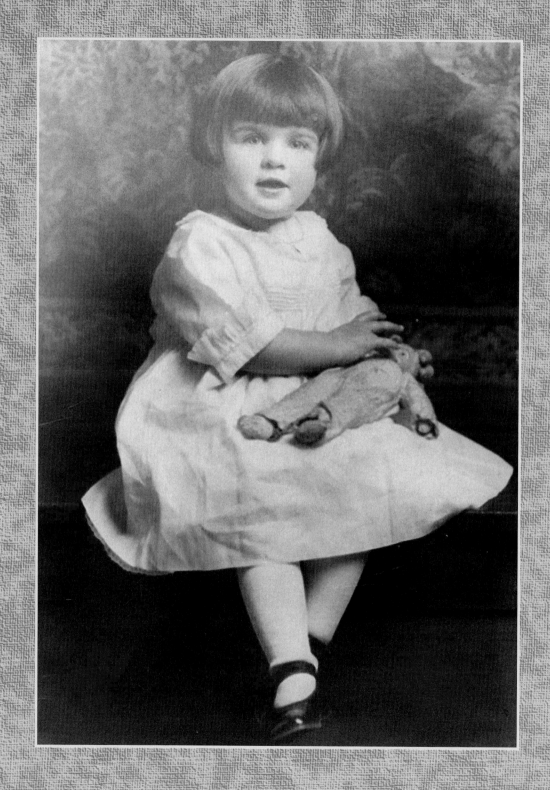

CHAPTER TWO

Sunny Days Ahead

✴ ✴ ✴ ✴ ✴ ✴ ✴ ✴ ✴ ✴ ✴ ✴ ✴ ✴ ✴

As a girl, Betty Ford would lie awake at night in bed and dream of dancing. And why not? Her girlhood was as sunny as could be, she said, with few cares and even fewer clouds to darken her days. Once a fortune-teller told her that when she grew up she would meet kings and queens. Betty thought the fortune-teller meant that she would meet great dancers, famous ballerinas, strong-limbed men who leaped gracefully across the stage.

For Betty, the fortune came true—she eventually did meet great dancers—but she also met real kings and queens. She had grown from little Elizabeth

✴ ✴ ✴ ✴ ✴ ✴ ✴ ✴ ✴ ✴ ✴ ✴ ✴ ✴ ✴

President and Mrs. Ford with King Hussein and Queen Alia of Jordan before a state dinner

President and Mrs. Ford with Japanese Emperor Hirohito and Empress Nagako in the Red Room

The Fords entertained Queen Elizabeth of Great Britain in July 1976.

Anne Bloomer in a small Michigan town to a tall, beautiful woman who was the First Lady of the land. As First Lady, she eventually entertained King Hussein of Jordan, Queen Elizabeth of Great Britain, the Emperor and Empress of Japan, and Queen Margrethe of Denmark.

But it wasn't her skills at entertaining or her taste in decorating for which she was esteemed, though they were impressive. Instead, it was her no-nonsense midwestern straightforwardness.

More than any First Lady before her, Betty Ford said what was on her mind. Sometimes it was just to family and friends. Often it was to the entire

Betty packing up the Alexandria household for the move to the White House

A 1974 photographic portrait of President and Mrs. Gerald R. Ford

nation, in a newspaper interview or on television.

When she experienced great joy, such as when her husband became president, or grave concern, such as when she announced to the world that she had breast cancer, Betty Ford was honest. She was unworried about the consequences because she believed that as long as she spoke the truth, nothing could go wrong. Be-sides, said Betty, the only reason she appeared to be so outspoken was that her predecessor in the White House, Pat Nixon, was so quiet.

Jerry Ford became president, as Betty had said, by accident, during one of the greatest political crises the

United States had ever weathered. For many years, he had been a congressman, traveling throughout the country and the world. He had never really aspired to be anything more. He had not run for president in the past, and he had not tried to become vice president, either.

Then, two years after Richard Nixon was elected to a second term, his administration started to fall apart. In order to avoid further loss of credibility after it became clear that his vice president, Spiro Agnew, would have to resign, the president looked to Congress and chose the man he thought represented the best of the best in America. That man was tall, conservative, and quiet. He had a reputation for honesty. He was Jerry Ford.

It had been a shock to Betty when Jerry was chosen, but she had survived shocks before. This was, as far as she was concerned, just one more twist in the long road they had traveled together as husband and wife. One more turn in a lifetime of turns that had shaped her, she thought, and enriched her.

She had been born in Chicago 55

Betty's mother, Hortense Neahr Bloomer, 1902

Betty's father, William Stephenson Bloomer, 1911

28

Portrait of America, 1918: The War to End All Wars

✫ ✫

By the year Betty was born, America included all its states except Alaska and Hawaii, and for the first time, more Americans lived in cities than anywhere else. The population numbered 103 million, and it is likely that all of them were talking about the First World War. Of course, no one called it that, because everyone believed that this horrible war would be the last ever. The Great War they called it, and it had raged in Europe since 1914. America sent troops to fight in 1917. By the time the war ended on November 11, 1918, well over 100,000 Americans had died. President Woodrow Wilson left for Paris in December to attend the peace conference.

Despite the happy news of the war's end, 1918 must have been a difficult year. As if the war weren't enough, a worldwide influenza (flu) epidemic at the same time took 500,000 lives in the United States and 20 million around the globe. Half the American soldiers who perished in Europe died of disease. Besides war and disease, Americans suffered through coal, oil, and gasoline rationing. They voluntarily observed "meatless" and "wheatless" days to help the war effort. In March, the government enacted daylight savings time to conserve energy. Grim though life was, patriotic Americans rolled up their sleeves and did their part. They knitted socks and hats for the soldiers and donated books for them to read. As the men went off to war, women took their jobs to keep the economy rolling.

In spite of the war, 1918 saw the fifteenth World Series, a game in which a young Babe Ruth pitched the American League Boston Red Sox to a 4-to-2 victory over the National League Chicago Cubs.

years earlier, in 1918. With her parents and two older brothers, she moved to Denver soon after her birth. When Betty was two years old, the family moved to Grand Rapids, Michigan. Her mother Hortense stayed home and tended to the children, expecting the best they could

Michigan, U.S.A.

✶ ✶

Though Betty Bloomer was born in Chicago, Illinois, she grew up in Grand Rapids, Michigan. This oddly shaped state in America's Midwest touches four of the five Great Lakes and has more shoreline than any state except Alaska. Its name comes from the Chippewa Indian word *Michigama* meaning "great lake." Two peninsulas and a multitude of islands make up the state's 58,200 square miles (150,738 square kilometers). While the Upper Peninsula remains mostly wild and wooded, the Lower Peninsula includes most of Michigan's large cities, including Detroit, "the Motor City"; Lansing, the state's capital; and Grand Rapids, Michigan's second-largest city and Betty's hometown. Grand Rapids was an early lumbering center, and when many Dutch and Polish craftspeople settled there in the 1800s, the city became famous for its furniture manufacturing. Since both Betty Bloomer and Jerry Ford grew up there, the Gerald R. Ford Museum is today located in downtown Grand Rapids.

achieve and always, under all circumstances, expecting good behavior.

Betty—no one called her Elizabeth except her parents, and that was only when they were angry at her—was the baby in a close-knit family. Each summer, the entire family would pack up the day after school ended for the year and head north to their house on

Hortense Bloomer, Betty's mother, with Betty's older brothers Robert (left) and William in 1916

One of Betty's most vivid childhood memories was of a terrible storm over the lake.

Whitefish Lake. There they stayed until the day before the new school year began. They swam, boated, and picnicked all summer long.

Betty, who was a chubby little girl, was known to wander away at family picnics, eating from other people's baskets. Finally, her mother hung a sign on her that said, "Do not feed this child." That seemed to work!

Times were simpler back then, and joy came from simpler activities. Betty's father, William Stephenson Bloomer, was a somber man who traveled widely as a salesman for the Royal Tire Company, selling conveyor belts to factories. He always brought Betty a present when he returned, and his homecomings were always happy occasions. He liked to play with old radio receivers called crystal sets, and when he would receive some distant station, no matter how fuzzy sounding the words or music, he would shout, "Wow! I got Chicago, I got Chicago, come listen to it!" and the family would run to gather around the radio.

One of Betty's most vivid memories of her summers at the lake happened during one of the worst storms

"Listening In"

✱ ✱

If you tickle a rock, will it whistle? The answer is yes, if the rock is a crystal and you tickle it with a wire. Amazingly, some crystals can pick up radio signals. The "cat whisker" detector—a fine wire placed in contact with a crystal—was a primitive way to "detect," or receive, radio signals and became the crucial part of early crystal radio sets. Building these no-power radio receivers became a popular hobby in the 1920s. Though KDKA, the first radio station with a permanent frequency, went on the air in 1920, many other experimental radio stations broadcast randomly over the airwaves. Few people had radios, but hobbyists constructed primitive receivers from a crystal, a cat whisker, a coil for tuning, and head-

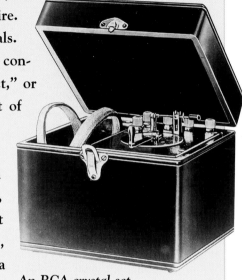

An RCA crystal set

phones. Such sets required no batteries, and they were inexpensive to build. Without set frequencies as a guide, crystal radio enthusiasts "listened in" to anything they could pick up. "Listening in" became a national pastime and gave Americans their first taste of the wonders of the electronic age that was soon to come.

she had ever experienced. "I can still feel my mother's arms around me, holding me, as she stood out on the porch and we watched a storm coming rolling in across the lake, waves swelling, thunder crashing, lightning slicing the sky, and my mother telling me how beautiful it was," recalled Betty. "I found out later she was scared to death, but she taught me not to be afraid."

She was, Betty later recalled, "safe in those arms."

Her mother taught her good manners, as well. Betty wasn't even allowed to butter an entire slice of bread before she ate it. Her mother said it was more polite to butter it in chunks and pull the bread apart as she ate. Nor could Betty eat an apple in her mother's presence. "You sound just like a horse," her mother would say.

That was about all the criticism Betty ever heard. In all other endeavors, she was encouraged. As a young girl, she recalled many years later, she was "a terrible tomboy and the bane of my big brothers' existence." She would follow them around trying to get into their football and hockey games, always begging to be included. It wasn't only that she wanted to be in on the fun, though. She enjoyed the physical involvement.

By the time Betty turned eight, her mother had steered her in a direction she thought more suitable for a young girl. Betty began dance lessons and quickly flourished. "My mother was a very strong person," Betty recalled, who encouraged her to excel at dancing. "I wanted to be as strong as she was."

Betty studied Spanish dance, tap, ballet, and acrobatics—and every type of dance she learned, she dreamed of dancing. "There was no kind of dance that didn't fascinate me," said Betty. "I'd hear about some boy who had been out West among the Indians and learned a rain dance, and I'd go to him and make him teach it to me."

At first, Betty studied ballet, which she found very difficult; that is, until she encountered contemporary dance. "I loved the freedom of movement it offered," said Betty. Besides, she said, "I was probably the worst ballet dancer that ever came down the road. I couldn't get my knees straight enough."

Still, while Betty was dancing each day, she still continued to play with her brothers and to have fun in other ways. On Halloween, for instance, when all the other kids went trick or treating, she and her friends would go on a rampage they called garbage night, in which they tipped over their neighbor's garbage cans, soaped their windows, and whitewashed their porches.

By the time she turned fourteen, she took her first real job—as a teenage model at Herpolsheimer's Department Store. "I would wander through

When Betty was fourteen (above), she took a job modeling at Herpolsheimer's Department Store.

Sixteen-year-old Betty catches a ball at an Ottawa Beach, Michigan, house party.

Herpolsheimer's tearoom wearing an outfit from stock, and ladies at the tables would stop me—'just one moment dear, let's look at that'—and I would say, 'twenty-five ninety-five, third-floor sportswear,' " said Betty.

As it had always been from the time she started taking lessons, dancing was still her first love. It was, she said, "my happiness." Though she was still taking dance lessons every day, she began to give dance lessons as well, every Saturday, charging neighborhood children 50 cents a lesson.

Overnight, it seemed, Betty had gone from being just a kid to being a young woman. "I was one of the fortunate people who slip into adolescence easily," admitted Betty, "turning from tomboy to girl without paying any particular price."

She concentrated more than ever on her dancing, even dreaming of becoming a professional. "I was looking ahead to a very important career as a dancer," she said. "I had aspirations, but I wasn't smart enough to have fears."

Fearless as ever, after graduating from Central High School at eighteen, Betty struck out on her own. She spent two summers in a row at the Bennington School of Dance at Bennington College in Vermont, studying dance with Martha Graham, one of the most extraordinary and famous dancers of all time. There, she said, she experienced the "ecstasy of being able to dance eight hours a day."

After her second summer away from home, Betty persuaded her mother to allow her to move to New York City for more study with Graham's dance troupe. She and a room-

At the age of eighteen, Betty Bloomer spent the summer at the Bennington School of Dance.

mate found an apartment and jobs— Betty modeled hats and furs and bathing suits in fashion shows—and danced and danced and danced.

"I used to take three subway trains to the job," said Betty, "marveling, as generations of girls have done, at the New York experience."

Still, though she was trying as hard

Martha Graham (1894–1991)

★ ★

Martha Graham was born on May 11, 1894, to Dr. George and Jennie Graham in Allegheny, Pennsylvania. Her parents moved with their three girls from that coal-mining region to California's sunny seacoast to help their middle daughter, Mary, overcome terrible asthma attacks. One day, at the age of sixteen, Martha stopped

in front of a window on a Santa Barbara Street, spellbound by a poster of famous exotic dancer Ruth St. Denis. Her fate was sealed. She studied at St. Denis's school, Denishawn, performing with its traveling dance company. At twenty-nine, she moved to New York City. She formed her own company, taught dance, and chore-ographed and starred in most of her works. Over her long career, she composed 170 dances. Greatly in-fluenced by native religious rituals and ancient legends, Martha not only created dances, she introduced new ways to dance. Her free, ab-stract style shocked audiences ac-customed to the grace and flow of ballet. She set her works to dissonant and unconventional music and engaged modern artists to create offbeat sets and cos-tumes. She danced until she was seventy-five and was suffering from arthritis. She taught, created dances, and directed her company until she died at the age of ninety-six, by then famous as the mother of modern dance.

Betty Bloomer (right) dancing at the Bennington College School of Dance during the summer of 1938

"The New York Experience"

★ ★

Young Betty Bloomer no doubt adored her "New York experience" in the late 1930s. Even as World War II loomed in Europe and the Great Depression caused economic hardship around the country, the lure of New York remained strong. The city promised a world of culture and excitement to those who were sturdy enough to survive its pace. The latest in modern painting and sculpture, literature, theater, and dance thrived there. Many artists and intellectuals fleeing Europe to escape the Nazis settled in New York in the late 1930s, injecting even more energy into the city's lively arts scene. Big-band swing music poured out of supper clubs and dance halls. The ultimate show in town during those years was the New York World's Fair, "The World of Tomorrow." Futuristic buildings and all the wonders of modern life—from nylon stockings to robots—spread over 1,200 acres (486 hectares) and attracted 44 million visitors. It was the biggest international fair ever mounted. New York deserved no less.

as she could to become a professional and "began to think I was ready to make whatever sacrifices it would take to be a concert dancer," she wasn't accepted into Graham's primary group of dancers, but into the second tier. Though Betty wasn't deterred by this, her mother, to some extent, was. She missed Betty very much and seized upon her second-class status at Graham's to persuade Betty to return home to Grand Rapids. "She never expected me to become so engrossed in this career," recalled Betty.

Her mother went to New York for a visit, chatting amiably about news from home, the parties that had been given, who was getting married to whom. Naturally, Betty became homesick.

Her mother finally asked Betty to come home for six months. If after that she still wanted to live in New York and pursue the life of a dancer, she would accept it and support her as best she could. "I'll never say another word against it," her mother promised. To Betty, that seemed like a reasonable offer.

In the back of her mind, Betty

Betty in 1938 at the age of twenty

knew she was leaving New York for good. Back in Grand Rapids, she again got a job at Herpolsheimer's, this time as assistant to the fashion coordinator. She arranged fashion shows, trained models, and designed the store window displays. At night, she taught dance and and started her own dance troupe, hoping, some thought, to become the Martha Graham of Grand Rapids.

Betty had a busy social life, too, and started dating Bill Warren, a man she had known almost all her life. "He was blond with curly hair, he was a good dancer, a good tennis player, he liked a good time, and unlike some of the men I dated, he wasn't a bit stuffy," said Betty. She found that she was falling in love.

Betty was twenty-four when she married Bill Warren in 1942. Yet, almost as soon as she finished saying her wedding vows, she knew in her heart that she had made a terrible mistake.

The Warrens moved often during the first two years of their marriage— from Michigan to Ohio and back to Michigan and then to Syracuse, New York, and then once more to Michigan, with Bill changing jobs each time. In Michigan, Betty went back again to Herpolsheimer's, now as *the* fashion coordinator, working with buyers and the advertising department, training models, putting on fashion shows, and traveling to New York to see the new styles.

Though they were finally staying

Betty Bloomer Warren dancing in Fantasy *in 1945*

This photograph of Betty (seated, second from left) with fashion models and other members of the Herpolsheimers' staff was taken in 1949.

put for a while, Betty became more and more unhappy in the relationship. While Bill was away in Boston on business, she began to write him a letter, explaining herself and asking for a divorce. Just then, however, Bill's boss phoned. Bill was sick, very sick, and could Betty fly to Boston?

"All of the time, the question kept snaking through my mind," Betty recalled many years later, "What am I doing here when I no longer love this man?" She felt, however, that she had no choice, so she took care of him day and night for two years. As soon as he recovered—he even returned to work—she filed for divorce.

With her new freedom, she delved into work, busying herself more than ever. So one night in August 1947, when a friend called trying to fix her up on a date with her friend Jerry, Betty at first said no. It was already late, and she was still working. Jerry got on the phone and persuaded Betty that one little drink—it would be less than an hour, he promised—wouldn't hurt. Betty finally accepted.

40

Jerry later said he had "no idea that someone special had just come into my life." Jerry Ford was twelve years older than Betty, a tall, handsome man who had been a football hero at the University of Michigan. He was still unmarried, having spent his time since graduating from Yale Law School concentrating on building his career. Betty knew of Jerry—after all, not that many authentic heroes lived in Grand Rapids—though she did not know him.

That first date led to another and another, and soon they were dating regularly. Though Jerry was shy and had a hard time expressing himself, he was ambitious, hungry to get into politics and make a name for himself. In fact, he was planning on running for Congress. Though he had big plans for his public life, Jerry was now beginning to form plans for his private life, as well. Increasingly, those plans included Betty.

No one was really surprised when Jerry asked Betty to marry him in February 1948. "He's a very shy man, and he didn't really tell me he loved me," said Betty. "He just told me he'd like

A photo of Gerald Ford taken during his 1948 campaign for Congress

to marry me. I took him up on it instantly, before he could change his mind."

First, Jerry told her, he had something important to do—to follow through on his dream, and to run for Congress. When he first told her, said Betty, she didn't really even know what running for Congress meant. "I was very unprepared to be a political wife," she said, "but I didn't worry because I really didn't think he was going to win."

As Betty continued to work at the department store and plan her wedding, Jerry ran a campaign. Betty volunteered, of course, putting up posters, licking stamps, and drafting all her friends to help. Jerry was a tireless campaigner, going from one speech to the next, from rally to rally to rally. Betty could barely keep up.

"After my initial misgivings, I got carried away by the momentum of the primary battle," Betty later admitted. "It was exhilarating to be in a race like

Gerald R. Ford (right) made a campaign stop at this Kent County, Michigan, farm.

that. You finally found yourself wanting him to win."

Even so, as election day neared, she saw less and less of Jerry. "The signs of what my future life was going to hold were there for me to read," she recalled years later. Even her sister-in-law had said that Betty would never have to worry about other women. "Jerry's work will be the other woman," she told Betty. Jerry even left their wedding rehearsal dinner to give a speech.

A *quonset hut campaign office*

Jerry left his and Betty's wedding reheasal dinner (below) to give a campaign speech.

The Fords leaving Grace Episcopal Church in Grand Rapids, Michigan, following their wedding on October 15, 1948

Gerald Ford (front right) at his wedding reception with his mother and stepfather and his half brothers Tom, Dick, and Jim Ford

Finally, Betty's wedding day arrived. She wore a sapphire blue dress and held a bouquet of red American beauty roses. Her shoes matched the dress and, on her hat, she fastened a piece of lace that had come from a parasol belonging to Jerry's grandmother. But where was Jerry? Campaigning, of course.

Betty was waiting in the doorway

The newly married Mr. and Mrs Gerald R. Ford (center) with their parents, Gerald R. Ford, Sr. and Dorothy Gardner Ford (left) and Hortense Neahr Bloomer Godwin and Arthur Meigs Godwin (right)

of the church at 4 o'clock on the afternoon of October 15, 1948, ready to go down the aisle, hoping that the man she was to marry would show up! "All of a sudden," said Betty, "he came flying in."

☆ ☆ ☆ ☆ ☆ ☆ ☆ ☆ ☆ ☆ ☆ ☆ ☆ ☆ ☆

CHAPTER THREE

Washington Wife

☆ ☆ ☆ ☆ ☆ ☆ ☆ ☆ ☆ ☆ ☆ ☆ ☆ ☆ ☆ ☆

Within a month of his wedding day, Jerry Ford won election to Congress, and he and Betty packed their bags for Washington, D.C. While Jerry had hundreds of other congressmen from whom to learn the rules of his new job, Betty had no one. Each politician's wife had to follow her own instincts, her own interests.

"I bought my first book on whether to wear gloves to a tea, and whether you take off one glove when going through a receiving line," said Betty, "and while these things seem silly sometimes, they make your life easier."

Her instincts and interests led to creating and raising

☆ ☆ ☆ ☆ ☆ ☆ ☆ ☆ ☆ ☆ ☆ ☆ ☆ ☆ ☆ ☆

House Rules

✮ ✮

Like the young Jerry Ford, each new representative in the U.S. House has many rules to learn. With 435 members, this half of the Congress (the other half is the Senate) needs order to keep business flowing along smoothly. All members therefore obey a set of rules called *parliamentary procedure*. The most popular guide to parliamentary procedure is *Robert's Rules of Order*, written by American army engineer Henry Martyn Robert in 1876 and based on the rules of Great Britain's Parliament. The rules are strict and complicated, so in the U.S. House of Representatives, a *parliamentarian* who understands the rules gives advice on how actions should take place. The Speaker of the House decides matters of procedure. To express their ideas, representatives must offer motions, and the Speaker controls who gets to speak, recognizing a representative before he or she can take the floor. No issue can even be debated before it is formally stated by the Speaker, and in a vote, the Speaker can break a tie in either direction, or create a tie that defeats the motion in question.

a family and being a good wife and mother.

Of course, she did all the usual things many of the other congressmen's wives did: she joined an organization of women called the Congressional Club, she visited hospitals, drove visiting Michiganders around the capital pointing out the sites, and even occasionally helped around Jerry's office.

In short order, however, she and Jerry created a family: Michael was born in 1950, John in 1952, Steven in 1956, and finally, much to Betty's delight, a daughter, Susan, in 1957.

Soon, Betty was helping around Jerry's office less often and instead was driving the children to and fro. "I was in the PTA. I was a den mother," Betty said. "I spent days in the car ferrying the children to the orthodontist

The Fords on the Capitol grounds after they arrived in Washington, D.C., in November 1948

Newlyweds Gerald and Betty Ford

This picture of Betty holding her infant son Jack while watching toddler Mike playing at a child's table was taken at the Fords' Alexandria, Virginia, home.

Betty, Jerry, and sons Mike and Jack admire Steve, the newest Ford, in 1956.

and the eye doctor." She was involved with the children's football and baseball teams, and she taught Sunday school at their local Episcopal church.

Their house, in suburban Alexandria, Virginia, was loud and raucous, with friends and neighbors often joining the Fords. At one time or another, the Ford family pets included gerbils, turtles, rabbits, a bird, and even chick-

Betty and Jerry with their children (from left) Steve, Mike, Jack, and Susan (in Jerry's arms) in the backyard of their home in Alexandria

ens. The presence of all these animals made life even more hectic.

Even amidst all the excitement and revelry, something was missing for Betty, and that something was Jerry. As his ambitions grew and he continued to win re-election every two years, so did his responsibilities grow. He traveled more often, and was away from home more than 200 nights a year. In fact, Betty counted 258 nights one year when Jerry did not come home for dinner. Other times, he worked all week and went directly

back to his district in Michigan for the weekend, never even stopping at home for a change of clothes.

"I couldn't say 'wait until your father comes home,' " recalled Betty of those years. "Their father wasn't coming home from work for maybe a week."

Even Jerry was aware of how his traveling affected Betty and the children. "It put a strain on the marriage," said Jerry. "I called every night . . . un-less a phone wasn't available, but I was all over the country, and sometimes overseas, and with four active children, Betty had a tough obligation. They were all doing their thing, and although they grew up to be nice kids, they had their problems, and she had to be not only the mother but the father."

Still, Betty reacted badly as his absence from the family intensified. "I was resentful of Jerry's being gone so

The Generation Gap

✫ ✫

As a mother of teenagers in the 1960s and 1970s, Betty Ford faced the same challenges as other parents all over America. While the 1960s began fairly quietly, the years after the assassination of President Kennedy in 1963 brought turmoil over the war in Vietnam, civil rights, and equality for women. Moved by these issues, American sons and daughters protested the war, demonstrated for desegregation, and demanded equal opportunities for men and women. A rebellious new youth culture grew out of this social activism. However, while the causes of peace and equality were good, the increasing drug use, political liberalism, disregard for authority, and sexual freedom that went along with the movement alarmed many parents. They hardly recognized their children—hippies and flower children who wore long hair, jeans, and tie-dyed T-shirts and listened to rock 'n' roll. At the same time, young people rejected their parents' clean-cut, conservative values. This division between older and younger Americans came to be known as the "generation gap."

It took wise parents and willing children to keep the gap from widening too far. The Fords encouraged their children to be independent thinkers. "They say what they think, and we've brought them up to have minds of their own," Betty said.

Congressman Gerald Ford (right) speaks to soldiers in South Korea during a 1953 congressional inspection tour.

Betty Ford (front left) with others aboard a naval launch at Pearl Harbor, Hawaii, in December 1968

much," admitted Betty. "I was feeling terribly neglected."

It didn't help matters that one night in 1964, while Jerry was asleep, she reached over the kitchen sink and strained her neck. The pain shot through her like a knife, yet she didn't want to wake Jerry. The next day, he took her to the hospital.

"My left arm had gone totally numb," said Betty. She remained at the hospital for several weeks, in traction. Unfortunately, she never fully recovered. To mask the pain, her doctors prescribed painkillers, which she took daily.

To the outside world, everything about the Ford family looked normal. On the inside, Betty was feeling lost and lonely. She needed someone to talk to, and began visiting a psychiatrist twice a week.

"I could tell him all the problems I couldn't talk to anybody else about," said Betty. She talked of her back pain, of her worries about drugs in the schools, of Jerry's being away so much, and of her loneliness. "Up until then, I'd thought I should be strong enough to shoulder my own burdens, not carry them to somebody else," Betty said. "I wasn't a woman who could run to her husband with 'The cook has quit,' when he came home tired and hoping for some tranquility."

For Betty, having someone to talk to proved to be very helpful. Her doctor not only listened, but urged her to take time for herself, to do things *she* liked to do. Betty recalled him telling her that if she "went to pieces" she would not be of much value to Jerry or the children.

"I don't believe in spilling your guts all over the place," said Betty, "but I no longer believe in suffering in silence over something that's really bothering you."

She had gained enough confidence to finally approach Jerry about her feelings and about her troubles. They spoke long and hard, and over much

President Nixon (center) during a 1971 meeting with Senate minority leader Hugh Scott, House minority leader Gerald R. Ford (right), and Congressman John Rhodes

Betty and Gerald Ford went deep-sea fishing during a vacation trip to Montego Bay, Jamaica, following the 1972 general election.

time, and eventually Jerry agreed to retire from politics when his current term—it was his twelfth—ended in 1974. Betty was relieved and began to plan for their new, quieter life.

But then, Vice President Spiro Agnew resigned. There was much speculation about whom the presi-

dent was going to choose to replace him. Jerry's name was on everyone's lips. Betty hoped the rumors were merely that. Then one night, while she and Jerry were spending a quiet evening at home, the phone rang. It was President Nixon.

"I've got good news," he said.

☆　☆　☆　☆　☆　☆　☆　☆　☆　☆　☆　☆　☆　☆　☆

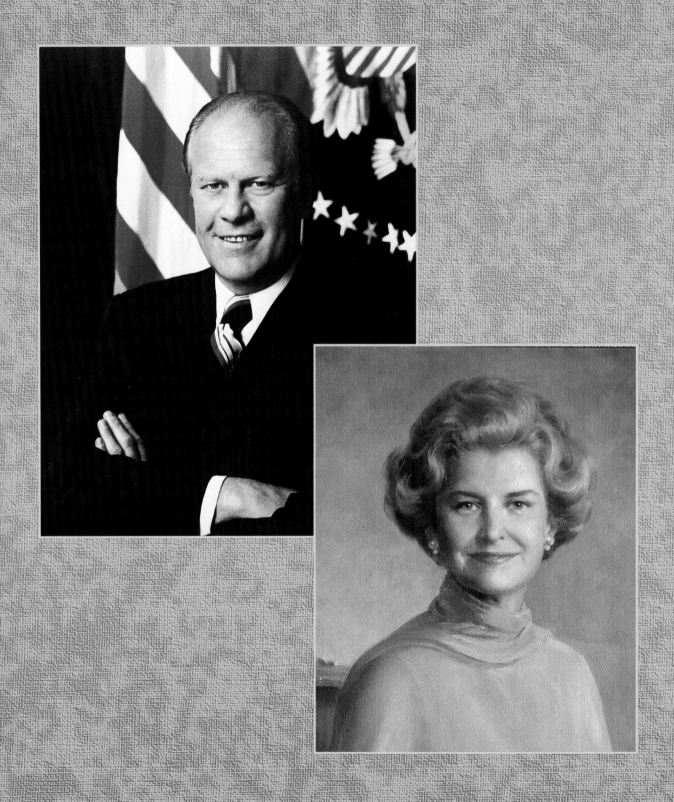

CHAPTER FOUR

Coming into Her Own

☆ ☆ ☆ ☆ ☆ ☆ ☆ ☆ ☆ ☆ ☆ ☆ ☆ ☆ ☆ ☆

If there was one thing Betty knew when she became First Lady, it was that she wanted to create a White House that was cheerful, informal, and comfortable. For the previous few years, it had been a gloomy place, with the Nixon presidency and family under siege. Betty sought to change that. It should be "an open, friendly White House" said Betty. "This home has been a grave. I want it to sing!"

Even *Newsweek* magazine said Betty was the type of First Lady who would "set a different style." The magazine said the White House under her control was "sure to be folksy."

☆ ☆ ☆ ☆ ☆ ☆ ☆ ☆ ☆ ☆ ☆ ☆ ☆ ☆ ☆ ☆

Betty Ford (right) hosted her first press conference as First Lady in the White House State Dining Room on September 4, 1974.

Betty agreed with that assessment. After all, she reasoned, though some former First Ladies had grand family heritages and others were accomplished public speakers and political activists, she herself was just a housewife who happened to be married to the president of the United States.

When Betty and Jerry entered the White House, there would be only two and a half years until the next presidential election, only two and a half years to make an impression on the country. Since she wouldn't be First Lady very long, she figured she

Susan Ford was photographed with Shan, the Ford family's Siamese cat, in October 1974.

President Ford, First Lady Betty Ford, son Steve, and daughter Susan feeding Flag, the deer, at Camp David in September 1974

might as well be forthright—what was there to lose?

Besides, the country had just gone through a difficult period—Nixon was the first president ever to resign from office—and the nation, it seemed, had lost all confidence in government's honesty. Betty wanted to show the people that you could be in govern-

ment and speak the truth. Betty would tell it like it is.

Her first challenge in living up to her personally set goal of being open and honest with the nation came only about a month after Jerry's swearing-in. Betty was diagnosed with breast cancer.

It was 1974. Breast cancer—in

After Betty's mastectomy at Bethesda Naval Hospital, she received this get-well card signed by all 100 U.S. senators.

Defeating Breast Cancer

✩ ✩

In the years since Betty fought her battle with breast cancer, many advances in identifying and treating the disease have been made. More women are learning to examine themselves for lumps and telltale signs to detect the disease early on. Doctors recommend routine *mammograms* (X rays of the breasts) for all women as they get older. New drugs and treatments give women more options. Experts are beginning to understand the importance of a diet rich in soy, grains, fruits, and vegetables in preventing breast cancer, along with the role that genetics and hormones might play in causing the disease. When doctors discovered that Betty Ford had cancer, their only choice was to remove the breast. Today, doctors are developing amazing new surgeries to remove as little as possible. Despite these advances, one in eight women will develop breast cancer, which is the second most common cancer among women and the second most deadly cancer among women aged forty to fifty-five. Without a cure, breast cancer remains a serious threat to all women.

fact, most types of cancer—was still a taboo subject. It was thought in many circles to be an unfit topic for public discussion. When Betty was told she had it, however, she knew in her heart that she would have to talk about it with the public, that people would want to know, and that what she had to say and what she would soon go through to regain her health, would be important.

Betty, wrote one reporter, was a "quiet crusader for frank and open discussion of what was once for closet conversation only."

Within days of speaking about it openly, and having a mastectomy, the White House was flooded with 55,800 get-well cards. It was then, for the first time really, that Betty realized the power of her influence, that as First Lady she could be a force for good.

Her honesty eventually persuaded millions of women to learn more about the risks of breast cancer—it had never before been so widely discussed. Millions more were encouraged to have an X ray exam called a mammogram, which could detect breast cancer. "I felt people were ask-

Jerry speaks to Betty in the hospital as Susan adjusts his cummerbund before a diplomatic reception.

Susan, Betty, Jerry, and Liberty on the way to the White House after Betty's release from the hospital

ing whenever I went in public: 'Which one did she lose?'" said Betty. "But I got over it by reminding myself how much good I'd accomplished."

Still, losing a breast in such a way was disheartening. Like other women, she admitted she was concerned about what she would look like afterward. It wasn't only vanity to worry about disfigurement, she thought, and it was important that the world—and especially other women—understood that.

"It is an honest concern," she said. "I started wearing low-cut dresses as soon as the scar healed and my worries about my appearance are now just the normal ones of staying slim and keeping my hair and makeup in order." When she asked herself whether she would rather have lost a right arm or a breast, she admitted, "I decided I would rather have lost a breast."

While Betty had received a lot of support and sympathy from around the country during her illness and the long recovery period, her relationship with the public was just really beginning. Soon after her operation, she held a press conference for 150 reporters in which she mentioned her

Betty, a strong supporter of the Equal Rights Amendment (ERA), is shown here wearing a "Ratify ERA in 1975" button.

support for the Equal Rights Amendment. It had already been ratified (approved) by thirty-five states, three states short of the number needed for it to pass and become a part of the Constitution. Betty told the group she not only supported it, but that she

The Equal Rights Amendment

* *

The Equal Rights Amendment that Betty Ford supported was never added to the Constitution. First written in 1923, it stated that men and women shall have the same rights under the law. The amendment was approved by Congress in 1972. To become law, it would need to be approved by 38 states by 1982. Thirty-five states approved the amendment before the deadline. Why would people vote against such a basic statement of equal treatment for men and women? Some feared that the amendment would force a negative change in the traditional roles of women. Many people believed that it would threaten family life and marriage. The industries that saved money by employing less-expensive female labor lobbied against the ERA. Some women believed they would lose protections already in the law if the ERA passed. Others were concerned about women being drafted into military service. A few even predicted that men and women would have to share public bathrooms. One critic, Phyllis Schlafly, organized an emotional campaign against the ERA. She reinforced all of these fears and took advantage of the fact that few Americans understood how the ERA would change their daily lives. In fact, women in states that adopted similar amendments to their state constitutions won victories in areas of equal pay, more varied work and educational opportunities, and property ownership.

would work to ensure its passage, whether it was by personally phoning state legislators around the country or merely talking about it with Jerry over dinner.

In fact, when a reporter asked her if she discussed her views with the president, Betty joked "If he doesn't get it in the office in the day, he gets it in the ribs at night." She called their nighttime conversations about political issues "pillow talk."

Supporting the ERA wasn't like supporting something everyone could agree on, such as the arts or handicapped children. Much of the nation

On August 29, 1974, a group of twenty-seven women presidential appointees met with President Gerald Ford and First Lady Betty Ford to offer ideas on how women could assume a larger role in government.

was against the amendment, and many people quickly turned on the First Lady. "Betty Ford is trying to press a second-rate manhood on American women!" complained many people.

Betty would not be deterred. She followed through on her commitment and began to phone state legislators asking them to support the amend-

ment. Some accused her of "arm-twisting" and others said the wife of the president should mind her own business, and not get involved with political issues. Protesters even paraded up and down in front of the White House. "Betty Ford, get off the phone!" read one sign.

Betty worked tirelessly on behalf of women's rights, even encouraging

First Lady Betty Ford shows off one of the 1975 White House Christmas trees.

First Lady Betty Ford and her daughter Susan work on homemade Christmas decorations in the White House solarium during the 1975 Christmas season.

Jerry to appoint women to high political offices. Though she fought to get a woman on the Supreme Court when one of the justices retired, for instance, Jerry instead named a man. Still, at her urging, he did appoint Carla Hills the first female secretary of housing and urban development and Anne Armstrong the United States ambassador to Great Britain.

The more Betty fought for women and the ERA, the more her activities turned into controversy. Once again, the White House was flooded with

President Ford appointed Carla Hills (left) the first female secretary of housing and urban development.

Ford appointed Anne Armstrong (below) the United States ambassador to Great Britain.

mail, both for and against her. At first, in fact, it was more against than for—three times as many people disagreed with her on these issues as agreed. Betty knew that if her words, especially about the ERA, had stirred up so much emotion, her message must be getting through. Secretly, she admitted, she was proud of the debate she had caused.

Once, after Jerry talked on television about his conservative views on abortion—which differed from her own—Betty slipped him a note that said, "Baloney! This is not going to do you a bit of good." Jerry didn't seem to mind. "I've been told I didn't play it

Madam Secretary

✫ ✫

The president's cabinet consists of twelve advisers, each picked by the president to head an important department in the government. The first woman cabinet member was Frances Perkins, appointed secretary of labor by President Franklin Roosevelt in 1933. She fought for child labor laws, minimum wages, and old-age pensions and spurred the passage of the Fair Labor Standards Act of 1935. When President Eisenhower created the Department of Health, Education, and Welfare in 1953, he appointed Oveta Culp Hobby its first secretary. She had organized and led the Women's Army Corp (WAC) during World War II. Carla Anderson Hills, President Ford's contribution to this list of honorable secretaries, served as secretary of housing and urban development. A distinguished trial attorney in California, Hills also served as an assistant attorney general of the U.S. Justice Department. President Carter was the first to appoint more than one woman to his cabinet, including Juanita Kreps, the first female secretary of commerce. Born to a poor family in a small coal-mining town, Kreps worked her way through school and specialized in labor economics. She also became the first woman director of the New York Stock Exchange. Women served under Presidents Bush and Reagan, and Bill Clinton was the first to name women to the key positions of secretary of state and attorney general. Once considered radical, today the idea of women in this exclusive circle of presidential advisers seems natural.

safe enough but my husband has always been totally supportive," she once said.

Betty wanted it understood that while she supported equal rights for women, what she really supported was the right of women to make choices for themselves, whether it was out in the work world or at home as a wife and mother. "Being a good housewife seems to me a much tougher job than going to the office and getting paid for it," she once said. "What man could afford to pay for all the things a wife

First Lady Betty Ford sits with pianist Van Cliburn, dance choreographer Martha Graham, and fashion designer Halston after a White House state dinner held in honor of Emperor Hirohito and Empress Nagako.

does, when she's a cook, a mistress, a chauffeur, a nurse, a baby-sitter? But *because* of this, I feel women ought to have equal rights, equal social security, equal opportunities for education, an equal chance to establish credit."

Betty was rarely out of the spot-light. In addition to her endorsement of the ERA, she supported the arts, hosting many famous musicians, actors, and dancers at the White House. Her passion for dance, in fact, never diminished. While she was First Lady, she even urged her husband to present

71

☆ ☆

President Harry Truman established the Presidential Medal of Freedom to honor those who gave notable service in World War II. In 1963, President Kennedy made it the highest honor that the U.S. government could award a civilian in peacetime. The award recognizes outstanding contributions in all walks of life from the arts and sports to civil rights and politics. Martha Graham was the first to receive the medal in the field of dance. More-recent recipients include tennis great Arthur Ashe, labor leader Cesar Chavez, Justices Brennan and Marshall of the Supreme Court, civil-rights leader Rosa Parks, and Frances Hessebein, former leader of the Girl Scouts of America.

the Presidential Medal of Freedom to her most respected and beloved former dance teacher, Martha Graham.

Betty was outspoken, to be sure, and clever and spontaneous, whether it was singing the University of Michigan fight song at a birthday party in her honor at Lincoln Center or pirouetting on stage after delivering a speech at a dance conference. Once, when she and the president were visiting China, she even danced in her stocking feet with a group of young

Martha Graham, Betty Ford's respected and beloved former dance teacher

First Lady Betty Ford danced in her stocking feet with a young ballet dancer at the Peking Dance School during a presidential visit to China.

At a Kansas City press conference, President Ford (right, next to his wife Betty) announced that Senator Robert Dole (left, next to his wife Elizabeth) would be his running mate in the 1976 presidential campaign.

First Lady Betty Ford is shown here during a controversial interview with Morley Safer of the television show 60 Minutes.

ballet dancers at their school. All the world was charmed.

No matter how entrancing she became, however, First Lady Betty Ford continued to be dogged by controversy. In 1975, only eleven days after her husband announced that he would run for a full term as president the following year, Betty accepted a request

for an interview from the television show *60 Minutes.*

She wasn't expecting a difficult interview; in fact, she thought the reporter, Morley Safer, would ask her easy questions, "softballs" they were called. She couldn't have been more wrong.

After an introduction, Safer asked

her what she thought about the Supreme Court's recent decision supporting the right of women to have abortions. Betty didn't cower, or try to think of what the best political—or least controversial—answer would be. She just said what was on her mind. The court's decision, she thought, was "the best thing in the world . . . a great, great decision."

What did she think of marijuana use by young people? Betty said had it been around when she was younger she would have tried it, too.

What did she think of premarital sex? While she didn't "personally favor it," she said, she admitted that it might decrease the number of divorces.

Finally, Safer asked her what she would tell her seventeen-year-old daughter Susan if Susan told her she was having an affair. Betty said she would counsel her daughter and want to know a lot about the boy. "She's a perfectly normal human being," said Betty.

While even today, these responses from the wife of the president might stir a great debate, in the mid-1970s they caused an uproar. Betty was once again in the center of the storm.

The White House was deluged with mail. More than 35,000 letters poured in, with at least 28,000 of them against Betty. One New Hampshire newspaper accused the First Lady of having "disgraced the nation." The immorality of her words was, the paper said, "almost exceeded by their utter stupidity. Involving any prominent individual this would be a disgusting spectacle. Coming from the First Lady in the White House, it disgraces the nation itself!"

A preacher in Dallas said he could not "think that the First Lady of this land would descend to such a gutter type of mentality!"

Betty stood behind her opinions. "I don't believe that being First Lady should prevent me from expressing my ideas," she said as a way of defense. "Why should my husband's ideas, or your husband's, prevent us from being ourselves?" Eventually the tide of public opinion began to turn her way. "At last," read one telegram sent to the White House, "a real First Lady."

First Lady Betty Ford (right) and singer Pearl Bailey (left), among sixteen women honored as the 1976 Women of the Year by the magazine Ladies Home Journal, do an impromptu dance at New York City's Ed Sulllivan Theater.

The Ford's son Steve, First Lady Betty Ford, and daughter Susan (wearing an "I Want Betty's Husband for President" button) chat at the 1976 Republican National Convention.

"Betty Ford should be banned from television," one journalist wrote. "She is too honest. Mrs. Ford wears her defects like diamonds. And they dazzle."

Her patience paid off. By November of the 1976 election year, public opinion polls showed more people supported her than didn't; by the end of the year, she was ranked the most admired woman in America. Even *People* magazine said she was one of the three most intriguing people in the country. *Newsweek* chose her as "Woman of the Year."

She garnered so much support, in fact, that though Jerry was the one running for election, campaign buttons started to appear saying, "Elect Betty's Husband. Keep Betty in the White House."

As Jerry's presidential campaign wore on, Betty became more involved, both physically and emotionally. She toured the country making appear-

An Occupational Hazard

✫ ✫

During his short presidency, Gerald Ford survived two assassination attempts. The unrelated attacks were both made in California in September of 1975, and both were carried out by women. Indeed, these were the first assaults on any American president by a woman. Neither Lynette Fromme nor Sara Jane Moore looked the part of a killer. Twenty-six-year-old Fromme, called Squeaky, was a small, child-like woman and a follower of mass murderer Charles Manson. On September 5, standing in a crowd of presidential well-wishers outside the California state capitol, Fromme took aim at Ford from 2 feet (61 cm) away. Had her gun fired properly, her plan would have been deadly. In San Fransisco three weeks later, Sara Jane Moore shot at Ford from across the street, missing him, and, miraculously, everyone else in the crowd. The forty-five-year-old Moore had led a checkered life as both a radical activist and an FBI informant and tried to kill Ford as "a protest against the system." Betty Ford took both close calls in stride, resigned to the dangers that her husband faced as president.

ances and speeches. Betty found that while she had not originally wished to become First Lady, once she moved into the White House, she enjoyed it. The White House, she said, altered her in essential ways. "I found the resources with which to respond to a series of challenges," she said.

She had blossomed, said the president's press secretary. Betty, he said, had come to the White House as a "silent, smiling plastic politician's wife," but she had become "an outgoing, witty, and warm public personality with strong and independent views."

Still, the pressure she felt along the campaign trail was taking its toll. She was still taking pain relievers for her back, and now she was taking other pills to relax her and help her to rest.

In fact, she found she couldn't get

President Gerald R. Ford and First Lady Betty Ford acknowledging sustained applause at the Republican National Convention on August 17, 1976

President Ford (left front) greets supporters at a riverboat during the 1976 presidential campaign.

along without drugs to get her through her days. The more she pushed herself, the more she had trouble continuing. Once, at a campaign rally where she gave a speech, she slurred her words and even referred to herself as president.

The campaign wound down and on election night, the family gathered to watch the results on television. It was a close race between Gerald Ford and Governor Jimmy Carter of Georgia. In the end, Carter squeaked by, winning the election. Betty was heartbroken. Jerry had wanted to win so much—and she had wanted him to win perhaps even more.

In the White House, Betty said, she had "flowered." Jerry wasn't away as much and, she added, "when I spoke, people listened. I could campaign for women's rights and against child abuse. I began to enjoy a reputation for candor, and was able to do

Jerry and Betty hugged each other while watching the election returns as they realized that Jimmy Carter, not Gerald Ford, would become the next U.S. president.

some good." Now, with the election over, all of that would be over, too. Betty admitted that she was bitter about the campaign's outcome.

After twenty-eight years of faithful service to the country, Betty thought the American people had made a big mistake by rejecting her husband.

"The truth is," Betty recalled, "I was at the end of my rope."

☆　☆　☆　☆　☆　☆　☆　☆　☆　☆　☆　☆　☆　☆　☆

CHAPTER FIVE

Life Goes On

★ ★ ★ ★ ★ ★ ★ ★ ★ ★ ★ ★ ★ ★ ★ ★ ★ ★

When Jerry lost the election in 1976, he and Betty decided not to return to their Alexandria home. That part of their life, they reasoned—the life of a politician and his wife—was over. They had accomplished what they could professionally, and they had raised the family there.

Losing the White House was a sign, perhaps, that they should move on. Together, they decided to build a house outside Palm Springs, California, from scratch, almost as a symbol of their looking forward to the future spent with family, friends, and even grandchildren.

At first, though, the future seemed dim. Jerry was

★ ★ ★ ★ ★ ★ ★ ★ ★ ★ ★ ★ ★ ★ ★ ★ ★ ★

The Spirit of '76

* *

Although 1976 brought defeat to the Fords, it also offered them a unique opportunity before they left office: to be the First Family of the nation for its bicentennial, or 200th birthday. The year-long celebration marked two centuries since the signing of the Declaration of Independence on July 4, 1776. The entire country joined in the party. Classrooms and communities, advertisers and songwriters from coast to coast caught bicentennial fever. Everything from beer cans to fire hydrants was dressed up in red, white, and blue. Hundreds of gifts poured into the White House from patriotic Americans, including the Declaration of Independence spelled out entirely in macaroni by a creative Wisconsin Girl Scout troop. On the Fourth of July, there were the usual parades, fireworks, and picnics, of course, but many extraordinary events took place as well. Six million people in New York watched a flotilla of historic tall ships cruise up the Hudson River. More than 10,000 immigrants became U.S. citizens in major cities across the nation. In George, Washington, residents baked a cherry pie measuring 60 square feet (5.6 square meters). Along a 455-mile (732-km) stretch of Interstate 80, works of ten U.S. sculptors were unveiled. Americans climbed mountains, ran marathons, and drove covered wagons halfway across the land in honor of the occasion. Besides giving speeches at Valley Forge and Independence Hall, President Ford opened a time capsule that had been sealed a century before on the nation's 100th birthday. It contained photographs and autographs of distinguished Americans. Betty Ford celebrated the bicentennial in Plymouth, Massachusetts, by attending the opening of an exhibit called "Remember the Ladies." The exhibit explored the lives of American women between 1750 and 1815. Its title came from the advice that Abigail Adams gave her husband John as he helped to create the new American government in 1776. "If particular care and attention is not paid to the ladies . . . ," she observed, "we will not hold ourselves bound by any laws in which we have no voice." Abigail became First Lady in 1797.

busy playing golf, serving on corporate and charity boards, and traveling around the country giving speeches. Betty, however, felt lost. The spotlight in which she had moved for almost three years was gone, and so too was her sense of direction.

"I'm restless," Betty said, remembering how dynamic she had been while First Lady "and I thrive on activity, maybe even struggle."

To cope with her loneliness and melancholy, Betty found herself drinking more alcohol and continuing more

An aerial view of the home in Palm Springs, California, leased by the Fords during the time their new home was being built

Though Jerry kept busy giving speeches and playing golf, Betty felt lost and depressed after her active White House years.

ented she appeared. She was incoherent sometimes and slurred her words. She wasn't eating, she didn't get dressed until late in the day, and she moped around the house.

It wasn't long before her family and friends became concerned. In fact, one of her best friends said she had been acting like a zombie.

"I found myself almost in the position of baby-sitting for her," said her daughter Susan. "She had no friends. You couldn't trust her. She wouldn't show up for appointments. I feared she'd fall and crack her head open. She was walking into a dead-end street."

Eventually, the Fords became so concerned they decided to confront her in something called an "intervention," where they would meet with her and try to persuade her that she needed help.

It was the beginning of April 1978. Jerry and Betty had been living in their new house for only two weeks. Betty was sitting on the green-and-white couch—her new couch of which she was so proud—when the entire family showed up, together with two doctors

than ever to depend on her painkillers. Together, the drugs and alcohol masked her troubles. She was fooling herself into thinking that no one noticed how depressed and disori-

President and Mrs. Carter hosted the Fords at the White House for the unveiling ceremony of the Fords' official portraits.

and a nurse. They told her why they were there. Instead of accepting their concern, Betty became angry.

She didn't want to hear *any* of what her family was telling her. "I was not on heroin or cocaine," Betty later wrote. "The medicines I took—the sleeping pills, the pain pills, the relaxer pills, the pills to counteract the side effects of other pills—had been prescribed by doctors, so how could I be a drug addict?

While the family was talking to her about drug dependency, Betty later admitted, she was hearing something quite different. She had been there for her children when they needed her, she had been there for Jerry, both as a wife and political campaigner. "They were saying 'Mother, you're sick, we love you and we want to help you,' " said Betty. "But what I heard was that I had let them down." Even worse, she remembered her own mother's words, "If you can't do it right, don't do it at all."

Betty was devastated. "You are all a bunch of monsters," she shouted at her family. "Get out of here and never come back."

But *this* time the family didn't listen. They returned not long after for another intervention. And this time it worked.

Alcoholics Anonymous: A Group Effort

☆ ☆

Alcoholics Anonymous (AA) began with two men who were struggling with alcoholism, a disease that causes addiction to alcohol. Both men, Bill W., a stockbroker, and Dr. Bob, a physician, understood that alcoholism was a disease of the emotions, body, and mind. They believed that recovered alcoholics could help other alcoholics become sober through group meetings. To develop their program, they put both of those ideas to work and formed an AA group at Akron's City Hospital in Ohio. A second group sprang up in New York and a third in Cleveland. From the beginning, AA was nonpolitical, nonprofit, and not associated with any church or cause other than to help people stop drinking. Members remain anonymous, and experiences shared at meetings are kept confidential. Alcoholics Anonymous spread like wildfire around the globe, and the concept has helped not only alcoholics and their families, but gamblers and people with eating disorders as well as other addictions.

"I think the intervention worked because we are so close," said Betty. "Even when the kids were small . . . we asked their opinions. . . . Any major decision has always involved all of us, and my recovery involved all of us, because my disease involved all of us."

As the intervention ended, the doctor asked if she was ready to go in for treatment. Betty said yes.

Jerry accompanied Betty to the Alcohol and Drug Rehabilitation Service of the Long Beach Naval Hospital in California. There, she was put in a room with three other women instead of a private room as she had demanded of the doctor. "Right off he was telling me, hey, lady, you may have been the wife of the president, but in here, you're nothing special," Betty recalled.

At Long Beach, she would meet other people in her same situation, join Alcoholics Anonymous, and begin her recovery. That first week, she shook so much without drugs and alcohol that, she said, "I didn't need an electric toothbrush." Betty finally admitted she was sick. "Now I had to change," Betty wrote later. "Or die."

Betty Ford leaving Long Beach Naval Hospital after her treatment for drug and alcohol dependency

Betty spent four weeks in the hospital learning to cope with her life as it really was, the ups and downs, the good and the bad. She thanked God for all that she had, and for the love she felt all around her. With so much support, she was able to get better, to

On October 6, 1978, three weeks after she had facelift surgery, former First Lady Betty Ford was honorary chairperson of a benefit performance and dinner for the American National Theatre and Academy.

regain her health. Now, she wanted to give back some of what she had learned. She wanted to support others in their time of need.

Over the next few years, Betty was active in fund-raising and planning the Betty Ford Center at Eisenhower Medical Center, near Palm Springs. It finally opened in October 1982, and is today one of the most well-thought-of alcohol and drug rehabilitation centers in the country.

"I am an ordinary woman who was called on-stage at an extraordinary

Betty in the Meditation Center at the Betty Ford Center for Treatment of Alcohol and Chemical Dependency at the Eisenhower Medical Center in Rancho Mirage, California, which opened in 1982

Betty meeting with new patients during a visit to the Betty Ford Center

First Lady Barbara Bush (standing right) with former First Ladies (from left) Lady Bird Johnson, Pat Nixon, Nancy Reagan, Rosalynn Carter, and Betty Ford at the dedication of the Ronald Reagan Presidential Library in November 1991

The Fords at the funeral of former president Richard Nixon on April 27, 1994

Former presidents (standing, from left) George Bush, Gerald Ford, and Jimmy Carter and former First Ladies (seated, from left) Lady Bird Johnson, Barbara Bush, Betty Ford, and Rosalynn Carter at the 1997 rededication of the Gerald R. Ford Museum. Ten new exhibits opened in what is one of the most innovative and technologically advanced president's museums in the nation.

Former First Lady Betty Ford at the age of seventy-six

Betty (age seventy-nine) and Gerald Ford share a meal in the dining room of their home outside Palm Springs, California.

time," Betty once said, recalling her years in the White House and those since. "I was no different once I became First Lady than I had been before. But, through an accident of history, I had become interesting to people."

As it turns out, she was more than merely interesting. Betty Ford helped people. Betty Ford, perhaps more than any First Lady before her other than Eleanor Roosevelt, *used* the power of what she called, "the office of First Lady."

☆　☆　☆　☆　☆　☆　☆　☆　☆　☆　☆　☆　☆　☆　☆

The Presidents and Their First Ladies

† wife died before he took office   ‡ wife too ill to accompany him to Washington   * never married

1885–1889			
Grover Cleveland	1837–1908	Frances Folsom Cleveland	1864–1947
1889–1893			
Benjamin Harrison	1833–1901	Caroline Lavinia Scott Harrison	1832–1892
1893–1897			
Grover Cleveland	1837–1908	Frances Folsom Cleveland	1864–1947
1897–1901			
William McKinley	1843–1901	Ida Saxton McKinley	1847–1907
1901–1909			
Theodore Roosevelt	1858–1919	Edith Kermit Carow Roosevelt	1861–1948
1909–1913			
William Howard Taft	1857–1930	Helen Herron Taft	1861–1943
1913–1921			
Woodrow Wilson	1856–1924	Ellen Louise Axson Wilson (1913–1914)	1860–1914
		Edith Bolling Galt Wilson (1915–1921)	1872–1961
1921–1923			
Warren G. Harding	1865–1923	Florence Kling Harding	1860–1924
1923–1929			
Calvin Coolidge	1872–1933	Grace Anna Goodhue Coolidge	1879–1957
1929–1933			
Herbert Hoover	1874–1964	Lou Henry Hoover	1874–1944
1933–1945			
Franklin D. Roosevelt	1882–1945	Anna Eleanor Roosevelt	1884–1962
1945–1953			
Harry S. Truman	1884–1972	Bess Wallace Truman	1885–1982
1953–1961			
Dwight D. Eisenhower	1890–1969	Mamie Geneva Doud Eisenhower	1896–1979
1961–1963			
John F. Kennedy	1917–1963	Jacqueline Bouvier Kennedy	1929–1994
1963–1969			
Lyndon B. Johnson	1908–1973	Claudia Taylor (Lady Bird) Johnson	1912–
1969–1974			
Richard Nixon	1913–1994	Patricia Ryan Nixon	1912–1993
1974–1977			
Gerald Ford	1913–	Elizabeth Bloomer Ford	1918–
1977–1981			
James Carter	1924–	Rosalynn Smith Carter	1927–
1981–1989			
Ronald Reagan	1911–	Nancy Davis Reagan	1923–
1989–1993			
George Bush	1924–	Barbara Pierce Bush	1925–
1993–			
William Jefferson Clinton	1946–	Hillary Rodham Clinton	1947–

Elizabeth Bloomer Ford
Timeline

1918	★	Elizabeth Bloomer is born on April 8
		United States and its allies win World War I
1920	★	Warren G. Harding is elected president
		Woodrow Wilson wins the Nobel Peace Prize
1921	★	White Sox players fix the World Series in the Black Sox Scandal
1922	★	Nineteenth Amendment, which gave women the right to vote, is added to the Constitution
1923	★	Calvin Coolidge becomes president upon the death of Warren G. Harding
1927	★	Charles Lindbergh makes the first nonstop solo flight across the Atlantic Ocean
		Babe Ruth hits 60 home runs
1928	★	Herbert Hoover is elected president
		Walt Disney releases the first Mickey Mouse animated cartoon
1929	★	Stock market crashes and the Great Depression begins
1931	★	"The Star-Spangled Banner" becomes the national anthem
1932	★	Franklin D. Roosevelt is elected president
		Amelia Earhart becomes the first woman to fly solo across the Atlantic Ocean
1933	★	Twentieth Amendment is added to the Constitution
		President Roosevelt begins the New Deal to end the Great Depression
1934	★	Nylon is invented
1935	★	Congress passes the Social Security Act
		Alcoholics Anonymous is organized

1936	★	Franklin D. Roosevelt is reelected president
1939	★	World War II begins
1940	★	Franklin D. Roosevelt is reelected president
1941	★	Japan bombs Pearl Harbor and the United States enters World War II
1942	★	Betty Bloomer marries William Warren
1944	★	Franklin D. Roosevelt is reelected president
1945	★	Franklin D. Roosevelt dies Harry S. Truman becomes president Germany and Japan surrender, ending World War II
1947	★	Jackie Robinson becomes the first African American to play major-league baseball Betty and William Warren are divorced
1948	★	Betty Bloomer marries Gerald R. Ford Harry S. Truman is reelected president Gerald R. Ford is elected to the U.S. House of Representatives
1949	★	United Nations headquarters is dedicated in New York City
1950	★	United States enters Korean War Michael Gerald Ford is born
1952	★	John Gardner Ford is born Dwight D. Eisenhower elected president
1953	★	Korean War ends
1954	★	Supreme Court declares segregated schools to be unconstitutional
1955	★	Rock 'n' roll music becomes popular
1956	★	Steven Meigs Ford is born Dwight D. Eisenhower is reelected president
1957	★	Susan Elizabeth Ford is born
1960	★	John F. Kennedy is elected president

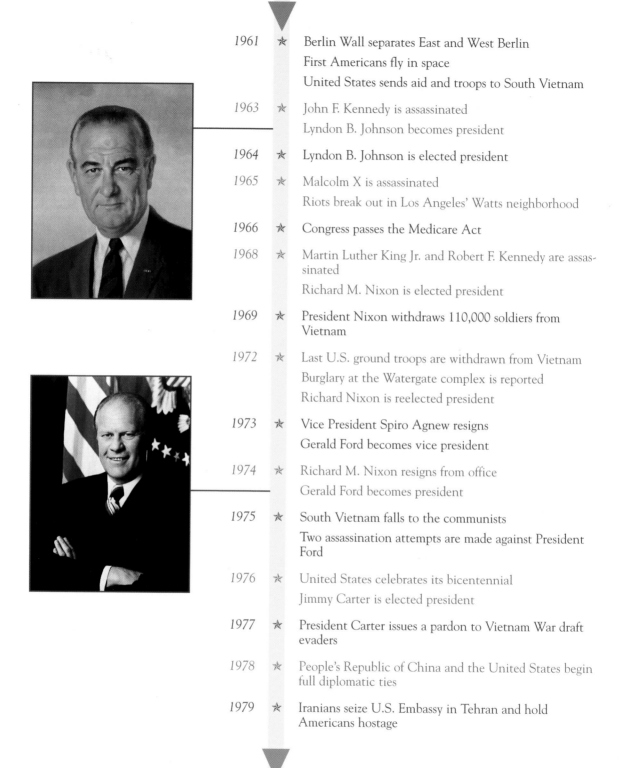

1961	★	Berlin Wall separates East and West Berlin First Americans fly in space United States sends aid and troops to South Vietnam
1963	★	John F. Kennedy is assassinated Lyndon B. Johnson becomes president
1964	★	Lyndon B. Johnson is elected president
1965	★	Malcolm X is assassinated Riots break out in Los Angeles' Watts neighborhood
1966	★	Congress passes the Medicare Act
1968	★	Martin Luther King Jr. and Robert F. Kennedy are assassinated Richard M. Nixon is elected president
1969	★	President Nixon withdraws 110,000 soldiers from Vietnam
1972	★	Last U.S. ground troops are withdrawn from Vietnam Burglary at the Watergate complex is reported Richard Nixon is reelected president
1973	★	Vice President Spiro Agnew resigns Gerald Ford becomes vice president
1974	★	Richard M. Nixon resigns from office Gerald Ford becomes president
1975	★	South Vietnam falls to the communists Two assassination attempts are made against President Ford
1976	★	United States celebrates its bicentennial Jimmy Carter is elected president
1977	★	President Carter issues a pardon to Vietnam War draft evaders
1978	★	People's Republic of China and the United States begin full diplomatic ties
1979	★	Iranians seize U.S. Embassy in Tehran and hold Americans hostage

1980	★	Ronald Reagan is elected president
1981	★	Iranians release the U.S. hostages
		Sandra Day O'Connor becomes the first woman appointed to the Supreme Court
1983	★	Sally Ride becomes the first American woman astronaut in space
1984	★	Ronald Reagan is reelected president
1986	★	Space shuttle *Challenger* explodes, killing all on board
1987	★	United States and Soviet Union sign nuclear missile reduction treaty
1988	★	George Bush is elected president
1989	★	Berlin Wall comes down
1990	★	Iraq invades Kuwait
1991	★	United States leads allies in Persian Gulf War
		Iraq is pushed from Kuwait
1992	★	Bill Clinton is elected president
1993	★	North American Free Trade Agreement is passed
1995	★	U.S. terrorists bomb the federal building in Oklahoma City, killing 168 people
1996	★	Bill Clinton is reelected president
1998	★	U.S. House of Representatives impeaches President Clinton
		Sammy Sosa (Chicago Cubs) hits 66 home runs and Mark McGwire (St. Louis Cardinals) hits 70
1999	★	U.S. Senate votes not to remove President Clinton from office
		NATO allies including the United States use air strikes on Yugoslavia to end "ethnic cleansing" in Kosovo
		President Clinton presents former president Gerald R. Ford with the Presidential Medal of Freedom

Fast Facts about
Elizabeth Bloomer Ford

Born: April 8, 1918, in Chicago, Illinois

Parents: William Stephenson Bloomer and Hortense Neahr Bloomer

Education: Graduated from Central High School, Grand Rapids, Michigan (1936); graduated from Calla Travis Dance Studio, Grand Rapids, Michigan; attended Bennington School of Dance, in Bennington, Vermont (summers of 1936 and 1937)

Careers: Model, dancer, and fashion coordinator and buyer

Marriages: To William Warren from 1942 until their divorce on September 22, 1947; to Gerald R. Ford from October 15, 1948, to the present

Children: Michael Gerald Ford, John Gardner Ford, Steven Meigs Ford, and Susan Elizabeth Ford

Places She Lived: Chicago, Illinois (1918); Denver, Colorado (1918–1920); Grand Rapids, Michigan (1920–1939, 1941–1942, 1944–1948); Bennington, Vermont (summers of 1936 and 1937); New York City (1939–1941); Ohio and Syracuse, New York (1942–1944); Alexandria, Virginia (1949–1974); Washington, D.C. (1974–1977); Palm Springs, California (1977–present)

Major Achievements:

⋆ Worked to increase the number of women in high government positions.

⋆ Worked to increase support for the arts, the handicapped, and the mentally ill.

⋆ Focused national attention on breast cancer when she talked openly about her radical mastectomy.

⋆ Established the Betty Ford Center for Treatment of Alcohol and Chemical Dependency.

⋆ Has received awards for her work on behalf of women's rights, examinations and treatments for cancer, and treatment for drug and alcohol dependence.

⋆ Encouraged her husband to present the Presidential Medal of Freedom to Martha Graham, her former dance teacher.

Fast Facts about Gerald Ford's Presidency

Term of Office: Served as the thirty-eighth president of the United States from August 9, 1974, to January 20, 1977, after Richard Nixon resigned the presidency because of the Watergate scandal

Vice President: Nelson A. Rockefeller (December 19, 1974–January 20, 1977)

Major Policy Decisions and Legislation:
* Granted an unconditional pardon to former president Richard Nixon on September 8, 1974.
* Offered plan granting conditional amnesty to draft evaders and deserters on September 16, 1974.
* Outlined an anti-inflation tax program on October 8, 1974.
* Signed a bill to expand unemployment insurance and job programs on January 4, 1975.
* Ordered helicopter evacuation of remaining Americans in Saigon, South Vietnam.
* Proposed statehood for Puerto Rico (December 31, 1976).

Major Events:
* Ford became the first incumbent president to visit Japan, where he met with the prime minister and the emperor on November 19, 1974.
* Carla Anderson Hills became secretary of housing and urban development on March 10, 1975, the only woman in President Ford's cabinet.
* The governments of Cambodia and South Vietnam fell to Communist forces (April 1975).
* Two assassination attempts were made on President Ford in September 1975: in Sacramento, California, by Lynette "Squeaky" Fromme, and in San Francisco by Sara Jane Moore.
* President Ford visited China (December 1, 1975).
* President Ford appointed John Paul Stevens as associate justice of the U.S. Supreme Court (December 19, 1975).

Where to Visit

The Capitol Building
Constitution Avenue
Washington, D.C. 20510
(202) 225-3121

The Gerald R. Ford Library
1000 Beal Avenue
Ann Arbor, Michigan 48109
Phone: (734) 741-2218
Fax: (734) 741-2341

The Gerald R. Ford Museum
303 Pearl Street NW
Grand Rapids, Michigan 49504-5353
Phone: (616) 451-9263
Fax: (616) 451-9570

Museum of American History of the
    Smithsonian Institution "First
    Ladies: Political and Public Image"
14th Street and Constitution Avenue
    NW
Washington, D.C.
(202) 357-2008

National Archives
Constitution Avenue
Washington, D.C. 20408
(202) 501-5000

The National First Ladies Library
The Saxton McKinley House
331 South Market Avenue
Canton, Ohio 44702

White House
1600 Pennsylvania Avenue
Washington, D.C. 20500
Visitor's Office: (202) 456-7041

White House Historical Association
740 Jackson Place NW
Washington, D.C. 20503
(202) 737-8292

Online Sites of Interest

The First Ladies of the United States of America

http://www2.whitehouse.gov/WH/glimpse/firstladies/html/firstladies.html

A portrait and biographical sketch of each First Lady plus links to other White House sites.

Gerald R. Ford Library and Museum

http://wwwlbjlib.utexas.edu/ford/

The Ford Library (in Ann Arbor, Michigan) and Museum (in Grand Rapids, Michigan) preserve and make available for research and public viewing the papers, audiovisual materials, and memorabilia of President Gerald R. Ford and First Lady Betty Ford. Includes links to general information about the library and museum, online photos and documents, reference services, museum programs, and more.

Internet Public Library, Presidents of the United States (IPL POTUS)

http://www.ipl.org/ref/POTUS/grford.html

An excellent site with much information on Gerald Ford, including personal information and facts about his presidency; many links to other sites including biographies and other Internet resources.

The National First Ladies Library

http://www.firstladies.org

The first virtual library devoted to the lives and legacies of America's First Ladies; includes a bibliography of books, articles, letters, and manuscripts by and about the nation's First Ladies; also includes a virtual tour, with pictures, of the restored Saxton McKinley House in Canton, Ohio, which houses the library.

The White House

http://www.whitehouse.gov/WH/Welcome.html

Information about the current president and vice president; White House history and tours; biographies of past presidents and their families; a virtual tour of the historic building, current events, and much more.

The White House for Kids

http://www.whitehouse.gov/WH/kids/html/kidshome.html

This site includes informtion about White House kids, past and present; famous "First Pets," past and present; historic moments of the presidency; several issues of a newsletter called "Inside the White House," and more.

For Further Reading

Clayton, L. *Barbiturates and Other Depressants*. New York: Rosen Publishing Group, 1994.

Clinton, Susan M. *First Ladies*. Cornerstones of Freedom series. Chicago: Childrens Press, 1994.

Devaney, John. *The Vietnam War*. New York: Franklin Watts, 1992.

Fisher, Leonard E. *The White House*. New York: Holiday House, 1989.

Fradin, Dennis Brindell. *Michigan*. From Sea to Shining Sea series. Chicago: Childrens Press, 1993.

Freedman, Russell. *Martha Graham: A Dancer's Life*. New York: Clarion Books, 1998.

Gormley, Beatrice. *First Ladies*. New York: Scholastic, Inc., 1997.

Gould, Lewis L. (ed.). *American First Ladies: Their Lives and Their Legacy*. New York: Garland Publishing, 1996.

Guzzetti, Paula. *The White House*. Parsippany, N. J.: Silver Burdett Press, 1995.

Kent, Deborah. *The White House*. Chicago: Childrens Press, 1994.

Kilian, Pamela. *What Was Watergate? A Young Reader's Guide to Understanding an Era*. New York: St. Martin's Press, 1990.

Klapthor, Margaret Brown. *The First Ladies*. 8th edition. Washington, D.C.: White House Historical Association,, 1995.

Mayo, Edith P. (ed.). *The Smithsonian Book of the First Ladies: Their Lives, Times, and Issues*. New York: Henry Holt, 1996.

Schlaadt, Richard G. *Alcohol Use and Abuse*. Grolier Wellness Encyclopedia. Guilford, Conn.: 1992.

———. *Drugs, Society, and Behavior*. Grolier Wellness Encyclopedia. Guilford, Conn.: 1992.

Sipiera, Paul P. *Gerald Ford: Thirty-Eighth President of the United States*. Chicago: Childrens Press, 1989.

Index

Page numbers in **boldface type** indicate illustrations

Photo Identifications

Cover: Portrait of First Lady Elizabeth Bloomer Ford by Felix de Cossio
Page 8: Betty Ford, wife of vice-president designate Gerald Ford, November 8, 1973
Page 24: Elizabeth Anne (Betty) Bloomer at the age of three
Page 46: Congressman Gerald R. Ford and his wife Betty on their way to a diplomatic party
Page 58: President Gerald R. Ford's official White House photograph; First Lady Betty Ford's official White House portrait by Felix de Cossio
Page 82: A post-White House portrait of Betty Ford

Photo Credits©

About the Author

Dan Santow is a former producer of *The Oprah Winfrey Show* and writer at *People* magazine. He is the author of *The Irreverent Guide: Chicago* (Frommer's/Macmillan, 1996) and has been published in many magazines, including *Redbook*, *Town & Country*, *Metropolitan Home*, *Men's Health*, *Chicago* magazine, the *Chicago Tribune Magazine*, and *Advertising Age*, among others. Mr. Santow is a graduate of Vassar College and holds a master's degree in journalism from Northwestern University. He lives in Chicago.